Kids Readers

Workbook and eBook

Level

3

Sandy Zerva

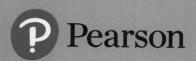

Contents

Book 1

Disney · PIXAR

TOY STORY 2

How do they feel?
Think and say.

2

Vocabulary

1 Find and circle. Then match the words (1–6) to the pictures (a–f).

1 __d__ apart**museum**r   **4** ____ casclombripdar

2 ____ cilpapartmented   **5** ____ veniatrcasedeter

3 ____ trarclimbadders   **6** ____ convaddressbel

2 Choose and write.

address   TV show   yard sale   camp

1 You can buy old things at a(n) _____.

2 Maria watches her favorite _____ every Friday.

3 Bill's _____ is 26, Maple Street.

4 We go to a(n) _____ in the summer. We have fun there!

3 Draw a shape to hide the extra letter.

1 f a e m o u s   **3** a p a r e t m e n t

2 m u s z e u m   **4** c l a i m b

Story

1 **Answer the questions.**

1 Does the man buy Woody at the yard sale? <u>No, he doesn't.</u>

2 Is Woody a famous toy? ....

3 Does Woody *really* want to go to Japan? ....

4 Does Andy like his new toys? ....

2 **How do Woody and Jessie feel at different stages in the story? Read and write.**

afraid   angry   excited   happy   sad   surprised

Beginning

4 Woody is <u>afraid</u> because <u>he is away from home</u>.

6 Jessie is .... because ....

Middle

8 Jessie is .... and .... because ....

12 Woody is .... because ....

End

19 Woody is .... because ....

20 Jessie is .... because ....

3 **Write about your favorite scene. Then talk about it.**

My favorite scene is on page .... I like it because ....

....

Language

1 🎧 **Listen and read.**

2 **Write** *was*, *wasn't*, *were*, *weren't* **or** *there*. **Use a capital letter where necessary.**

1 Maria: There _____was_____ (✔) a space ranger in the toy box. There _____ (✘) a doll.

Louis: _____ there a toy truck in the box?

Maria: No, _____ _____. (✘)

2 Dylan: There _____ (✔) some color pencils in the basket. _____ _____ (✘) any pens.

Julia: _____ _____ any coloring books?

Dylan: Yes, _____ _____. (✔)

3 **Talk about the picture. Look and remember. Then cover and play.**

Was there a doll in the picture?

No, there wasn't.

5

Phonics

1 🎧 **Listen and circle. Which sound do you hear, x or y?**

1
x
y

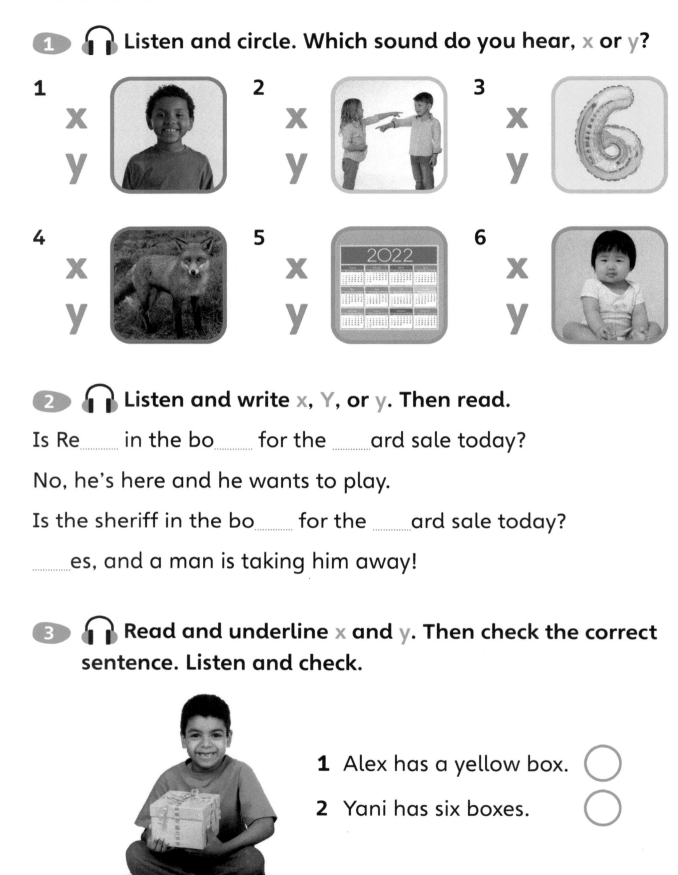

2
x
y

3
x
y

4
x
y

5
x
y

6
x
y

2 🎧 **Listen and write x, Y, or y. Then read.**

Is Re____ in the bo____ for the ____ard sale today?

No, he's here and he wants to play.

Is the sheriff in the bo____ for the ____ard sale today?

____es, and a man is taking him away!

3 🎧 **Read and underline x and y. Then check the correct sentence. Listen and check.**

1 Alex has a yellow box. ◯

2 Yani has six boxes. ◯

Values: Friendship

1 **Choose and answer.**

1 Who are Woody's friends? ....

2 Who is a new friend? ....

3 Who helps Woody to go back home? ....

 **a**  **b**  **c**  **d**  **e**

2 **What makes a good friend? Rate these things from 1–5. Add one more thing.**

	Not important → Very important				
	1	**2**	**3**	**4**	**5**
We like the same things.	○	○	○	○	○
My friend is kind.	○	○	○	○	○
My friend is funny.	○	○	○	○	○
My friend helps me.	○	○	○	○	○
My friend is smart.	○	○	○	○	○
....	○	○	○	○	○

3 **Share.**

My best friend's name is Ruby. She's funny! She helps me with my math homework.

Find Out

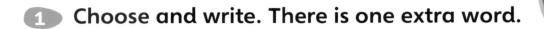

1 **Choose and write. There is one extra word.**

farms   gold   wagons   rivers   the West   ranches

1 In the 1800s, people moved to .... of the US.

2 They arrived there with .... and horses.

3 They lived on small ...., but their life wasn't easy.

4 Cowboys and cowgirls worked on ....

5 Some people looked for .... in California.

Writing tip

***The cows walked** in front of **the cowboy**.*

Use a preposition to say where things are.

2 **Write. Put the words in the correct order. Use a capital letter and a period.**

1 a / to / big house / the / small house / next / there's

....

2 horses / see / two / in / can / the / of / I / front / big house

....

3 are / there / behind / two houses / more trees / the

....

Game Follow the Path

Start

1 Say it.

Where was Andy?

2 Spell it.

......ellow bo......

3 Correct two mistakes.

In the 1900s, many people moved to the American West. They used cars to get there.

6 Say it.

Was there a truck in the story?

5 Spell it.

a back ......ard

4 Say it.

What can you see at an airport? Name two things.

7 What is it?

Are all Andy's toys famous?

8 Say it.

9 Say it.

What is it?

10 Say it.

What is Woody doing?

Finish

Now I can...

- ◯ understand some words for places and travel.
- ◯ ask and say where things were in the past.
- ◯ read and write words with x and y, and say their sounds.

9

Book 2

Disney

101 DALMATIANS

What are the dogs doing?
Think and say.

Vocabulary

1 **Read and circle words about dogs.**

crash   spots   bark   village   fur   puppy   snow

2 **Label the pictures.**

spot   village   fur   inside   fall in love   outside   snow

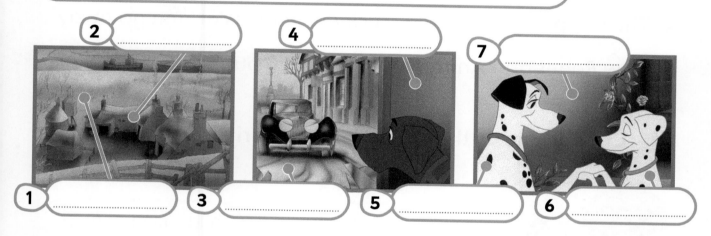

2 ....

4 ....

7 ....

1 ....

3 ....

5 ....

6 ....

3 **Do the crossword.**

1 not inside

2 a baby dog

3 people speak; dogs ....

4 you are in the same class

5 frozen water; it falls from the sky

6 animal hair

Story

1 **Read and circle.**

1 Cruella De Vil is Anita's old **classmate / teacher**.

2 Cruella wants **the puppies for pets / to make a fur coat**.

3 There are more **farm animals / Dalmatian puppies** in Cruella's house.

4 The puppies jump into **a truck / Cruella's car** and go away.

5 Now Roger and Anita have **101 / 116** puppies!

2 **Choose one of the characters and write a profile.**

Description	Personality
tall short thin eyes hair fur	bad kind smart brave angry

Character profile   Name ....

Description .... is ....

.... has ....

Personality .... is ....

I know this because ....

3 **Imagine you are a character in this story. Who do you want to be? Why?**

I want to be .... because ....

Language

1 🎧 **Listen and read.**

💬 Language

How many stars **are** there?   There **are a lot of** stars.
How much snow **is** there?   There**'s a lot of** snow.
How much water **is** there?   There**'s a little** water.

2 **Read and circle.**

1 John: How **many / much** birds are there?

Tan: There are **a lot of / a little** birds.

2 Maya: How **many / much** ice is there?

Sophia: There's **five / a little** ice.

3 Jill: How **many / much** clouds are there?

Kat: There's **one / a little**.

4 Abby: How **many / much** dirt is there?

Sam: There's **a lot / many**.

3 **Practice the language. Talk about the pictures. Use these words and your own.**

animals dogs ice mountains
people plants trees snow water

Phonics

1 🎧 **Listen and check the words you hear.**

1
- shirt ◯
- short ◯

2
- far ◯
- fur ◯

3
- bored ◯
- bird ◯

4
- hurt ◯
- hot ◯

5
- first ◯
- fast ◯

6
- moving ◯
- morning ◯

2 🎧 **Listen and write** ar, ir, or, ur. **Then read.**

B_____ds in the p_____k.

A h_____se in the d_____k.

A dog with c_____ly f_____

St_____ts to b_____k.

3 🎧 **Read and underline** ar, ir, or, **and** ur. **Then check the correct picture. Listen and check.**

1 Marni has a purple skirt.

 ◯  ◯  ◯

2 This store sells sports clothes.

 ◯  ◯  ◯

Values: Courage

1 **Who is showing courage? Check.**

1 ◯ The men are looking for the puppies.

2 ◯ Tibs is hiding the puppies.

2 **Do the quiz. Choose a, b, or think of your own answers.**

1 You are late for school. You see a young boy in the street. He is lost.

   a You stop and see how you can help.

   b You don't stop. You don't want to be late.

2 One of your friends tells a lie.

   a You don't want to fight with your friend. You keep quiet.

   b You ask your friend to tell the truth.

3 Some older children want to fight with your friend. Your friend is scared and doesn't want to fight.

   a You tell them to go away.

   b You walk away.

3 **Share.**

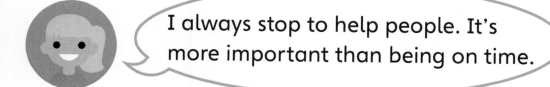

I always stop to help people. It's more important than being on time.

Find Out

1 **Read and check True or False.**　　**True**　**False**

1 Dogs can smell and see very well.　　○　○

2 People can hear better than dogs.　　○　○

3 Chocolate is bad for dogs.　　○　○

4 We call a dog's fur a "jacket".　　○　○

5 There are many different kinds
of dog.　　○　○

Writing tip

There are five dogs and fifteen cats.

In lists, we write numbers as numerals (5). In
sentences, we can write numbers as words (five).

2 **Do the puzzle. Write the numbers as words.**

In a room, there are four children and their
pets: a parrot, a dog, a cat and a duck.

1 How many heads? There are _____ heads.

2 How many legs? There are _____

3 How many arms? There _____

4 How many eyes? _____

Game Spin the Wheel

Yes or No?

10 People wear coats. Dogs have coats, too.

Choose.

1 Roger and Anita **crash / fall** in love.

Say it.

9 How much dirt is there? There is _____ dirt!

Show it.

2 bark

Spell it.

8 c _____ ly
f _____

3 The g _____ l is b _____ ed.

Spell it.

Say it.

7 Sam and Jen are in the same class. They're _____ .

4 What's happening?

Say it.

6 Are they inside or outside?

5 How _____ spots _____ there?

Say it.

Say it.

Now I can...

- ◯ understand some words for feelings, dogs, and nature.
- ◯ ask and answer questions with *How much* and *How many*.
- ◯ read and write words with ar, or, ir, and ur, and hear their different sounds.

17

Book 3

Disney

Tangled

What is different about
Rapunzel's hair? Think and say.

Vocabulary

1 **Choose and write. There is one extra word.**

> guard   tie   golden   crown   cut

1 ....   **2** ....   **3** ....   **4** ....
hair

2 **Unscramble the words. Then match them to the pictures.**

1 s o t e r f   **2** n e r t n s l a   **3** e r t a   **4** e t i

....

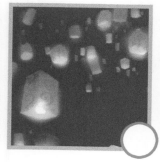

3 **Put the words in the correct circle.**

1
.....tree.....

.....forest.....

2
....

....

3
....

....

4
....

....

tree   forest   street   city   castle   tower   sun   sky

Story

1 **Read and circle a or b.**

1 Why does Rapunzel leave the tower?

    a To follow her dream.   **b** She hates her life there.

2 Why does Flynn give the crown to the Stabbingtons?

    a Because people are more important than things.

    b Because he is afraid of the brothers.

3 Why does Flynn cut Rapunzel's hair?

    a To take her magic.   **b** To free her from Mother Gothel.

2 **Where do these scenes take place? What is happening?**

1   tower

2   ....

3   ....

4   ....

1 Rapunzel is ....

2 Rapunzel is ....

3 Flynn is ....

4 Rapunzel and her parents are ....

3 **Think about Rapunzel's life. Write.**

Her life inside the tower is ....

Her life outside the tower is ....

20

Language

1 🎧 **Listen and read.**

> ## 💬 Language
>
> **How often** do you walk to school?
>
> I **never** walk to school.
>
> never ⟶ sometimes ⟶ usually ⟶ always

2 **Put the words into the correct order to make dialogs.**

1 Marie: you / often / do / go to the park / how /?

....

Alex: go to the park / I / on the weekend / usually /.

....

2 Ben: do / often / TV / you / how / watch /?

....

Claire: TV / watch / in the evening / I sometimes /.

....

3 **Practice the dialog. Make questions and give true answers.**

go to the movies

have dinner with your family

listen to music

have English class

21

Phonics

1 🎧 **Listen and number.**

| bang ◯ | sing ◯ | ping ◯ | thing ◯ |
| bank ◯ | sink ◯ | pink ◯ | think ◯ |

2 🎧 **Listen and write ng or nk. Then read.**

Rapunzel is home. It's the first day of spri........

We're having a party, in front of the Ki........

Let's have a dance, enjoy food and dri........

Is Rapunzel excited? What do you thi........?

3 🎧 **Read and underline ng and nk. Then match. Listen and check.**

a The elephant is pink.   **c** Thank you!

b Bring me that book, please.   **d** Good morning!

1

2

3

4

Values: Positivity

1 **Choose the correct answer.**

Rapunzel is never bored in the tower. Why?

a She thinks of the world outside the tower.

b She does a lot of things.

c She looks out of the window.

2 **Are your hobbies on this list? Check (✔). Add your hobbies.**

1 ( ) I draw or paint.   **5** ( ) I dance.

2 ( ) I play games.   **6** ....

3 ( ) I make things.   **7** ....

4 ( ) I play music.

3 **Share.**

I usually play my guitar after school, and I sometimes draw pictures.

Find Out

1 **Match the captions to the pictures.**

a Reading light in the old days

b Reading light these days

c Lantern festival in China

d Lanterns in Hawaii

Writing tip

Why **did they use lanterns?**

They used lanterns *because* **they didn't have electricity.**

Use *because* to answer *Why* questions.

2 **Choose and complete the sentences. Start with *because*.**

they want to remember the brave people   it is dark
they can use them in festivals   they make a beautiful light

1 People like lanterns ....

2 People make paper lanterns ....

3 People put lanterns in the ocean in Hawaii ....

....

4 People use lanterns at night ....

Game Connect Three in a Line

1 Spell it.

Can you bri ___ ___ me that book?
Tha ___ ___ you!

2 Which is the odd one out?

city

guard

street

3 Say it.

How often are there lanterns in the sky?

4

Why do people like lanterns today?

5 Say it.

___ do you ___ lunch with your friends?

6 Spell it.

I thi ___ ___ this answer is wro ___ ___ .

7 Say it. Use the same word.

Rapunzel has ___ hair.

The king wears a ___ crown.

8 Say it.

What heals Flynn?

9 Say it.

Where is Mother Gothel's tower?

Now I can ...

○ understand some words for places and people.

○ ask and answer questions with *How often*.

○ read and write words with nk and ng, and hear their different sounds.

a bug's life

Disney · PIXAR

Does Princess Atta like Flik's invention? Think and say.

Vocabulary

1 Circle the words. Find the secret message.

Flafraidikfightisrealasticksmacircusrtscareant

Secret message: _____

2 Match the sentences (1–5) to the words (a–e).

1 A big bug with strong back legs. It can jump high.

2 You do the wrong thing. It's a _____.

3 A small bug. It works hard.

4 You _____ in a school play.

5 A thing scares you, so you are _____.

a perform

b mistake

c afraid

d grasshopper

e ant

3 Complete the words. There is one extra piece.

 grass cir  ge  per  take

1 mis

2  hopper

3 to  ther

4 cus

Story

1 **What happens next? Read and check.**

Flik goes to the city to find some help. He comes back with the circus bugs.

1 The circus bugs have a plan to stop the grasshoppers, but it doesn't work. Then a real bird fights the grasshoppers and they run away. ◯

2 Flik has a plan to stop the grasshoppers, but it doesn't work. The ants and the circus bugs get together to fight the grasshoppers and they run away. ◯

2 **Why do the characters do these things? Write.**

What the characters do.	Why do they do it?
1 The ants collect food for the grasshoppers.	Because the ants are scared of the grasshoppers.
2 The circus bugs agree to go to Ant Island.	
3 The ants and the circus bugs make a bird with sticks and leaves.	
4 The grasshoppers run away from Ant Island.	

3 **Look at this scene. What do you think the characters are saying?**

Language

1 🎧 **Listen and read.**

> ### 💬 Language
>
> The frog is **smaller than** the bird.
> This bug is **more beautiful than** that bug.
> Is the butterfly **prettier than** the flower? Yes, it is.

2 **Write. Use the correct form of the words.**

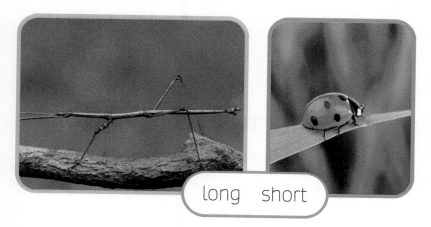

long   short

1 The stick bug is

_____

than the ladybug.

2 The ladybug is

_____

than the stick bug.

3 This bug is _____ than the grasshopper.

4 The grasshopper is

_____ the bug.

colorful   noisy

3 **Compare the bugs and animals. Use these words and your own.**

bee   butterfly   frog   fish   ant

Phonics

1 🎧 **Help Flik get to the city. Listen and circle k or qu.**

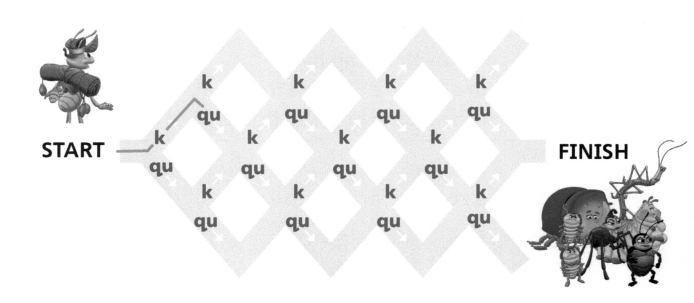

START

k qu k qu k qu k qu

k qu k qu k qu k qu

k qu k qu k qu k qu

FINISH

2 🎧 **Listen and write k, Qu, or qu. Then read.**

Look at Fli_____.

He wants a ball to _____ick.

The _____ind _____een,

Has a ball for Fli_____.

_____ick, Fli_____,

Give it a _____ick!

3 🎧 **Read and underline k and qu. Then draw. Listen and check.**

The queen is drinking her milk quickly and the king is asking her a question.

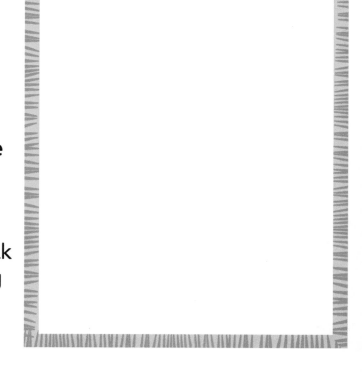

Values: Teamwork

1 **Read and check (✔).**

Flik, the ants and the circus bugs get together to fight the grasshoppers. Who is stronger now?

The grasshoppers ◯

The ants ◯

2 **Choose and write. Add one more thing. Then check the two most important things for you.**

time   ideas   fun   stronger   faster   easier

We can
do things
.... ◯

We have
more
.... ◯

Teamwork

....
.... ◯

We are
.... ◯

The work is
.... ◯

It is
.... ◯

3 **Share.**

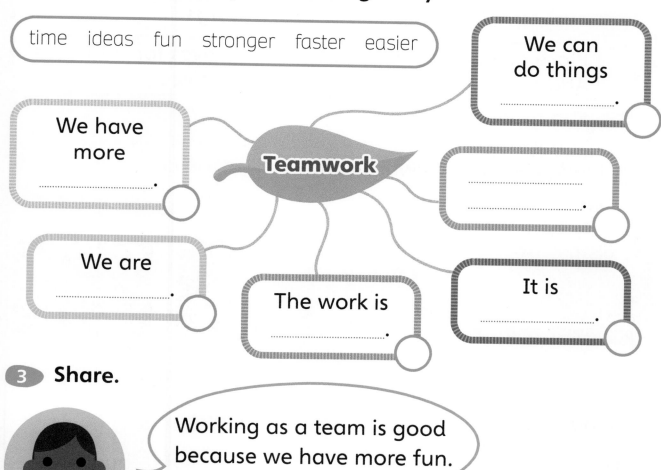

Working as a team is good because we have more fun.

Find Out

1 **Ants or grasshoppers? Write *a* or *g*.**

1 They have six legs and four wings. ....

2 They can carry things that are heavier than they are. ....

3 They can make a noise. ....

4 They don't have ears. ....

5 They live and work together. ....

6 They can jump high. ....

> ### Writing tip
>
> **Ants are** *small, brown* **bugs.**
>
> Place adjectives for size before adjectives for color.
> Add a comma between the two adjectives.

2 **Look, choose two words and write. Use these adjectives.**

> big   long   small   brown
> green   pink   red

1 A grasshopper is a .... bug.

2 A ladybug is a .... bug.

3 This isn't a flower. It's a .... bug!

4 This is a .... butterfly.

Game Follow the Path

Start

1 Say it.

Do ants have eyes and ears?

2 Say it.

Together, the ants are .... the grasshoppers.

3 Spell it.

The ants wor .... ickly.

4 Say it.

What do the circus bugs want to do? What does Flik want them to do?

6 Say it.

Bigger or smaller? Make two sentences.

5 Happy or tired?

In the beginning, the ants are ....

In the end, the ants are ....

7 Describe the birds.

What's the difference?

8 Show it.

I'm afraid.

9 Spell it.

This is a .... iz.

10 Say it.

What is it? What do the ants use to make it?

Finish

Now I can...

◯ understand some words for insects and feelings.

◯ compare two things.

◯ read and write words with k and qu, and say the sound.

Why are the characters happy? Think and say.

Vocabulary

face paint __2__

stage _____

skull _____

guitar _____

skeleton _____

2 **Do the crossword.**

1 Abuelita _____ Miguel's guitar because she is angry.

2 Miguel finds Ernesto's
guitar inside his _____.

3 Miguel plays the guitar.
He wants to be a _____.

4 Miguel walks on the
flower _____
with his dead family.

```
          1
          s
   2
   t
          3
          m
4
b
```

3 **Put the words in the correct group.**

| skull | guitar | skeleton | song | singer | tomb | stage | dead | musician |

Music

Día de los Muertos

35

Story

1 **Answer the questions.**

5 What happens next?

1 Where is Miguel?

2 When does this happen?

4 What does he see?

3 Why does he take the guitar?

2 **What do we know at the beginning of the story, and at the end? Write the numbers.**

1 The Rivera family don't play or listen to music.

2 There's always music in the Rivera family home.

3 Mama Coco remembers her father.

4 Coco's father loved music more than his family.

5 Ernesto was a bad person. He poisoned Hector.

6 Ernesto is Miguel's favorite musician.

Beginning
....
....
....

End
....
....
....

3 **Do you agree with Miguel's actions? Check.**

		I agree	I don't agree
1	3 He does not listen to Abuelita. He plays music.	◯	◯
2	6 He runs away from his family.	◯	◯

Language

1 🎧 **Listen and read.**

> ### 💬 Language
>
> What **did** you **do** today?
>
> I **walked** to the park.
> We **played** soccer.

2 **Put the verbs in the past tense.**

Fred: What did you do today?

1 Tina: I _____ (email) my friends.

I _____ (invite) them to my party.

2 Bea: I _____ (listen) to music and

I _____ (dance). I _____ (love) it!

3 Lee: My friends and I _____ (watch) a funny

movie on TV. We _____ (laugh) a lot!

3 **Practice the dialog. Use these words and your own ideas.**

skate in the park

wash the dog

help my (brother/sister/friend)

watch a movie

plant some flowers

finish my book

Phonics

1 🎧 **Listen and match 1–6 to a–f.**

1	**2**	**3**	**4**	**5**	**6**
br	fl	sk	dr	sm	pl

a	**b**	**c**	**d**	**e**	**f**
ate	art	ush	ant	oor	ink

2 🎧 **Listen and write the s-, l-, and r- blends. Then read.**

Miguel walked back from that beautiful ....ace

With a song in his head and a ....ile on his face.

Across the ....ower ....idge to see

His ....andmother and his family.

The ....eletons all look down and say,

"That boy can sing, that boy can ....ay!"

3 🎧 **Read and underline the s-, l-, and r- blends. Then check (✔) the correct picture. Listen and check.**

1 The yellow plant with green leaves is in a brown pot.

2 The sky is blue and the plane is flying over the clouds.

Values: Self-belief

1 **Correct the sentences. Change the underlined words.**

In the beginning, Miguel was <u>happy</u> to go on stage. ....

On stage, he wasn't afraid. He played <u>badly</u>. ....

In the end, the skeletons <u>hated</u> him. ....

2 **Put the sentences in the correct list. Add your own ideas.**

Your friend did something but it didn't go well. He/She is afraid to try again. What do you say to help?

1 You can do this!

2 You're not good!

3 It didn't go well but it's OK. You can try again.

4 You can learn how to do this.

5 This is very difficult. You can't do it.

6 You can't do this. Don't try again.

Things that help 👍	Things that don't help 👎
....	....

3 **Share.**

When my friend is afraid to try again, I tell him: You can do this!

Find Out

1 Match the sentences (1–5) to the words (a–e).

1 The Día de los Muertos is	**a** shrines.
2 On that day, families remember	**b** Mexico City.
3 There's a big parade in	**c** a happy day.
4 People leave food and drinks on	**d** dead people.
5 To come back to this world, the dead follow	**e** orange flowers.

☰ Writing tip

***On November 2nd*, *people celebrate the Día de los Muertos*.**

Write the month, then the day.

Use ordinal numbers for dates: first = 1st, second = 2nd, third = 3rd, fourth = 4th

2 Complete the sentences. Write the dates.

Halloween
10/31

Valentine's day
02/14

Earth Day
04/22

1 People celebrate Halloween on ....

2 Valentine's Day is on ....

3 Earth Day ....

4 My birthday ....

Game Spin the Wheel

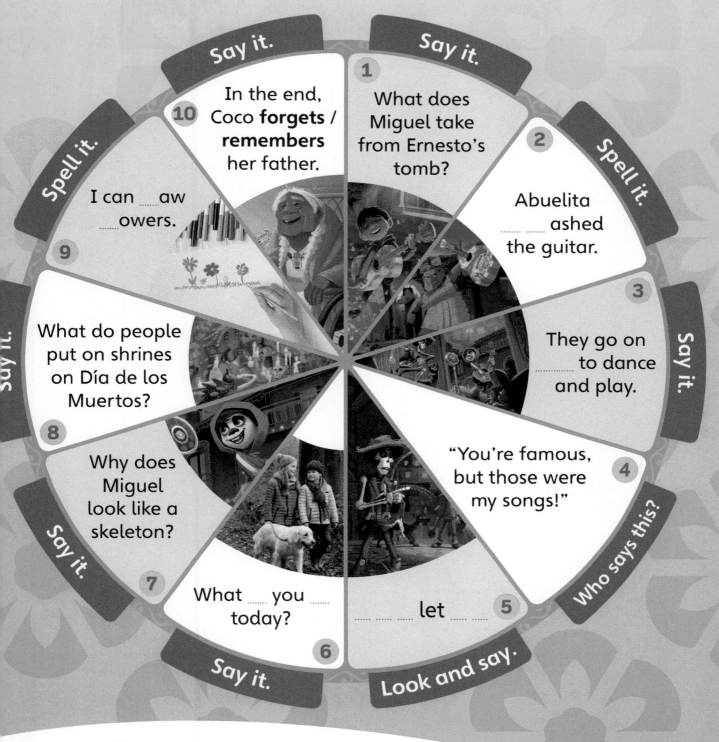

Say it. (top left)
10 In the end, Coco **forgets** / **remembers** her father.

Say it. (top right)
1 What does Miguel take from Ernesto's tomb?

Spell it.
2 Abuelita _____ _____ ashed the guitar.

Say it.
3 They go on _____ to dance and play.

Who says this?
4 "You're famous, but those were my songs!"

Look and say.
5 _____ _____ _____ let _____ _____

Say it.
6 What _____ you _____ today?

Say it.
7 Why does Miguel look like a skeleton?

Say it. (left)
8 What do people put on shrines on Día de los Muertos?

Spell it.
9 I can _____ aw _____ owers.

Now I can ...

○ understand some words for music and festivals.

○ ask and say what I did today.

○ read and write words with sk/sm, fl/pl, and br/dr, and hear the different sounds.

DISNEY
FROZEN II

What can you see? What can't
you see? Think and say.

Vocabulary

1 **Find the words.**

b	m	a	p	u	a	p	a	m	h
e	r	g	y	g	m	i	s	t	o
a	g	j	n	r	a	o	k	c	s
r	g	s	c	a	r	f	l	f	n
t	g	g	i	c	e	s	q	i	o
h	f	n	b	a	c	t	o	r	w
q	n	a	t	u	r	e	r	e	z

2 **Match the sentences (1–4) to the answers (a–d).**

1 Where's the village? ....

2 I'm cold. ....

3 There's lots of snow! ....

4 I can't see the mountain. ....

a Let's make a snowman!

b I don't know. Let's look at the map.

c It's because there's a lot of mist.

d Take my scarf. It's warm.

3 **Make word pairs. What do they have in common?**

1 snow ....

2 fire ....

3 map ....

4 nature ....

5 glacier ....

(fire)   (ice)

(light)   (dam)

(scarf)   (north)

(year)   (mist)

(river)   (voice)

Story

1 **Read and check (✔) the sentences which are true.**

1 Anna and Elsa want to help people. ◯

2 Their parents never tell them about the Northuldra. ◯

3 The spirits can talk to Anna. ◯

4 Elsa and Anna's grandfather was not a good person. ◯

5 Anna does a brave thing. ◯

2 **Write one word to describe each setting in the story. Then put the settings on the timeline.**

The town

pretty

The glacier

....

The castle

....

The forest

....

The dam

....

The sea

....

Beginning ⟶ 1 .... ⟶ 2 ....town....

5 .... 4 .... 3 ....

6 .... 7 .... ⟶ End

3 **Which is your favorite setting in the story? Why?**

I like ....

Language

1 🎧 **Listen and read.**

> 💬 **Language**
>
> **Can** you **come** to my house?　　No, I **have to do** my homework.

2 **Complete the dialogs.**

1 Vin: .... a video game?　**we / play**

　Zara: No, we have to go home now.

2 Jamie: Can you wear a dress to school?

　Mika: No, ... pants.　**we / wear**

3 Dan: .... to the park with us?　**Lucy / come**

　Sophie: No, she has to help her mom.

4 Luke: Can I do this work tomorrow?

　Teacher: No, ... it today.　**you / finish**

3 **Practice the dialogs. Use these words and your own ideas.**

　ride my bicycle to school?　　play some music?

　　stand up?　　use my phone?

be quiet

put it in your bag

sit down

take the school bus

Phonics

1 🎧 **Listen and check the words you hear.**

1
chop	◯
shop	◯

2
much	◯
mush	◯

3
chip	◯
ship	◯

4
chair	◯
share	◯

5
watch	◯
wash	◯

6
chew	◯
shoe	◯

2 🎧 **Listen and write ch or sh. Then read.**

Elsa _____ows Anna

The _____apes in the snow.

_____e tou_____es them,

_____e wat_____es them,

And Anna _____outs, "Oh!"

3 🎧 **Read and underline ch and sh. Then match. Listen and check.**

1 There's a sandwich in the kitchen.

a

2 There's some cheese in the kitchen.

b

3 Charlie is my pet fish.

c

4 Sasha is my pet chick.

d

Values: Resilience

1 **Which picture shows Anna being strong? Check.**

2 **Do the quiz. Then count the answers.**

1 A thing is difficult to do, so …

   a I stop trying.

   b I try more.

2 A thing doesn't work, so …

   a I find other ways to do it.

   b I do the same thing again and again.

3 When I'm scared of doing a thing, I think …

   a 'I'm strong!'

   b 'I'm not strong!'

4 There is a problem, so …

   a I try to make things better.

   b I don't think about it.

5 When I don't understand things, …

   a I ask questions.

   b I forget about them.

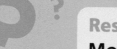

Results:
More As: You are strong like Anna!
More Bs: You can be stronger if you try!

3 **Share.**

Sometimes, I'm strong. But sometimes, I'm a bit lazy and I stop trying!

Find Out

1 **Read and circle.**

1 Glaciers are big **oceans / rivers / mountains** of ice.

2 We use a lot of **ice / water / glasses** from glaciers.

3 An iceberg is **69% water / a glacier / a big piece of ice**.

Writing tip

Glaciers move all the time, *but we can't see this with our eyes.*

> Use *but* to link two contrasting sentences.
> Add a comma before *but*.

2 **Match the sentences. Then join them into one sentence.**

a A long time ago glaciers covered 32%.

b You can find some glaciers on mountains, too.

c Some glaciers move very fast.

d Glaciers are often blue!

1 A lot of glaciers are near the sea ....

2 Glaciers cover about 10% of the Earth ....

3 Small pieces of ice are white ....

4 Glaciers are very heavy ....

Game Connect Three in a Line

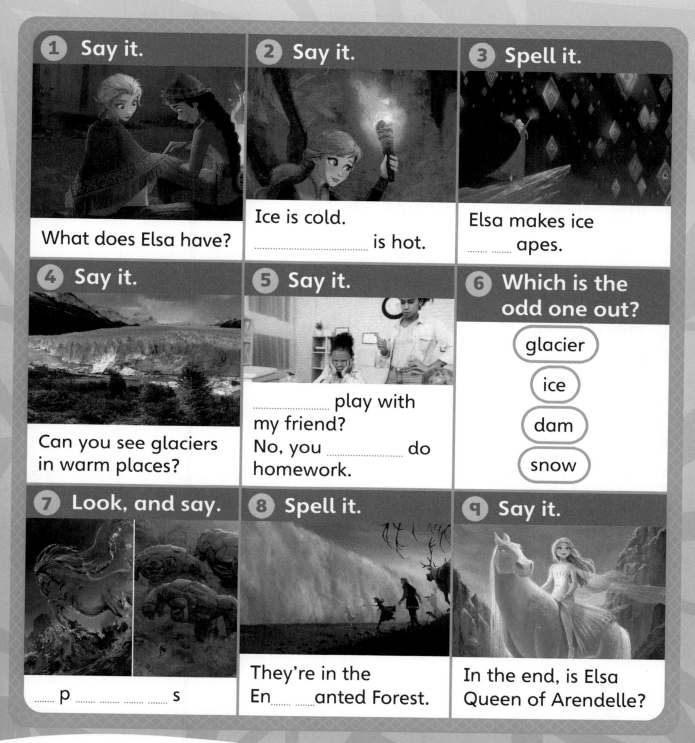

1 Say it.

What does Elsa have?

2 Say it.

Ice is cold.
_____ is hot.

3 Spell it.

Elsa makes ice
___ ___ apes.

4 Say it.

Can you see glaciers in warm places?

5 Say it.

_____ play with my friend?
No, you _____ do homework.

6 Which is the odd one out?

glacier

ice

dam

snow

7 Look, and say.

___ p ___ ___ ___ s

8 Spell it.

They're in the En___ ___anted Forest.

9 Say it.

In the end, is Elsa Queen of Arendelle?

Now I can...

○ understand some words about nature.

○ ask if I can do things and say what I have to do.

○ read and write words with ch and sh, and hear their different sounds.

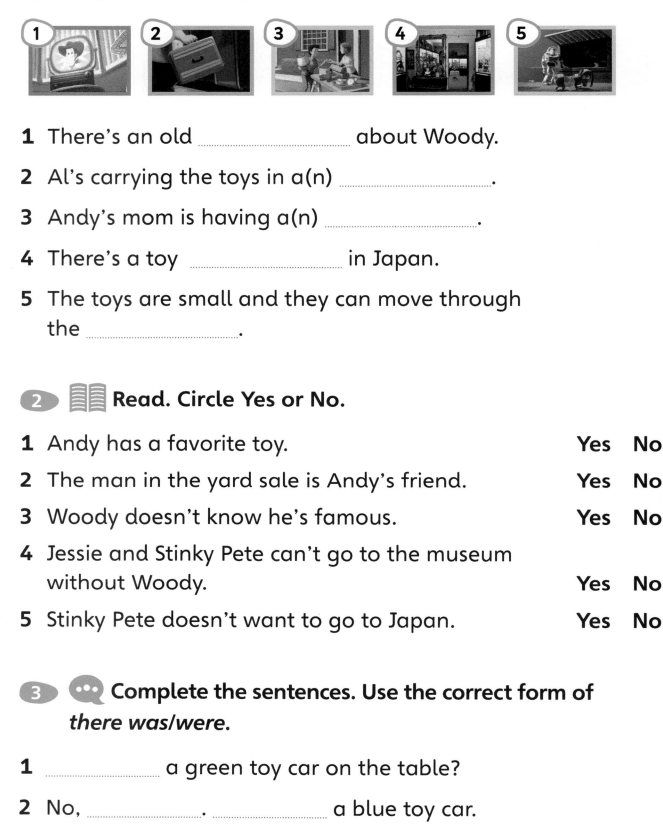

1 Ⓐ ⓐ **Look at the pictures and write the word(s).**

1 There's an old .... about Woody.

2 Al's carrying the toys in a(n) ....

3 Andy's mom is having a(n) ....

4 There's a toy .... in Japan.

5 The toys are small and they can move through the ....

2 📖 **Read. Circle Yes or No.**

1 Andy has a favorite toy.   **Yes   No**

2 The man in the yard sale is Andy's friend.   **Yes   No**

3 Woody doesn't know he's famous.   **Yes   No**

4 Jessie and Stinky Pete can't go to the museum without Woody.   **Yes   No**

5 Stinky Pete doesn't want to go to Japan.   **Yes   No**

3 💬 **Complete the sentences. Use the correct form of there was/were.**

1 .... a green toy car on the table?

2 No, ... a blue toy car.

3 .... a picture of Woody in the book?

4 Yes, ... But .... a picture of Buzz.

1 Aa Look and write the words.

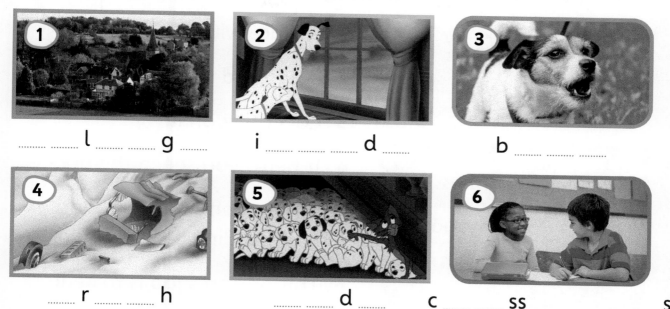

1 .... l ...... g ......

2 ...... i ...... d ......

3 b ....

4 ...... r ...... h

5 .... d ......

6 c .... ss .... s

2 Read and circle.

1 Perdita doesn't **like / know** Cruella De Vil.

2 Two **men / dogs** take the puppies away from their home.

3 Tibs helps the puppies get out of Cruella's **car / house**.

4 Cruella **crashes / loses** her car. She can't follow the puppies.

3 Look, read, and write. Use *How much/many, a lot of, a little* and numbers.

1 .... dogs are there?

There are .... dogs.

2 .... horses are there?

There are .... horses.

3 .... snow is there?

There's ....

1 **A a Match the words (a–f) to the sentences (1–6).**

a lantern

b city

c crown

d guard

e forest

f street

1 A place with a lot of trees. ....

2 Kings and queens wear it. ....

3 Cars drive on it. ....

4 It helps you see in the dark. ....

5 A place with a lot of people and buildings. ....

6 This person's job is to keep danger away. ....

2 **Match the actions (1–3) to the themes (a–c).**

1 Rapunzel leaves the tower to see the world. ....

2 She becomes more important to Flynn than the crown. ....

3 Flynn cuts her hair to free her from Mother Gothel. ....

a People can change.

b Protect the people you love.

c Follow your dreams.

3 **Write the question or the answer.**

1 .... listen to music?

I usually listen to music in the evening.

2 How often do you watch TV?

.... (never)

3 .... ?

We sometimes go to the movies at the weekend.

1 **Aa** **Look and write the words.**

1 .... t

2 .... c .... s

3 r l

4 m .... s .... a ....

5 t .... g e .... h ....

2 **Read and write. Use one word.**

On Ant Island, the **1** .... work all day to find food
for the **2** .... Flik goes to the **3** .... to find
some help. He comes back with the circus bugs. **4** ....
has a plan to stop the grasshoppers, but it doesn't work.
The ants and the circus bugs get together to **5** ....
the grasshoppers. In the end, the grasshoppers **6** ....
away.

3 **Read and write. Use these adjectives.**

1 big   The fish is .... the frog.

2 beautiful   This bird .... that bird.

3 long   The caterpillar .... the ladybug.

4 noisy   The frog .... the bee.

5 fast   The ant .... the stick bug.

1 [A][a] Read and check (✔) or cross (✗).

1 The man is a musician. ◯

2 They are in a tomb. ◯

3 Mamá Coco is a skeleton. ◯

4 There's a photograph on the wall. ◯

5 Miguel is wearing face paint. ◯

6 They are playing music on a bridge. ◯

2 Read. Circle Yes or No.

1 Ernesto de la Cruz played music in movies. **Yes No**

2 Miguel sees Ernesto in Mamá Coco's family photo. **Yes No**

3 Miguel can see and talk to dead people. **Yes No**

4 Hector has family in Miguel's world. **Yes No**

5 Hector poisoned Ernesto. **Yes No**

3 Read and write the verbs in the correct forms.

1 What did you _____ today?

I _____ my dad with the shopping.

2 What _____ yesterday?

We _____ a funny movie.

1 🅰🅰 **Read and match. Write the words.**

nature   fire   scarf   earth   map   snow

1 You can wear it on a cold day. ....

2 Frozen water. It falls from the sky. ....

3 It's very hot. ....

4 You look at this to find a place. ....

5 Animals, plants, and oceans are part of it. ....

6 Trees grow on it, and we live on it. ....

2 📖 **Read and circle.**

1 Anna and Elsa want to **meet** / **help** people.

2 The spirits can talk to **Anna** / **Elsa**.

3 The Northuldra didn't like the **Arendellians** / **Spirits**.

4 Anna **does a brave thing** / **doesn't know what to do**.

3 💬 **Read and write. Use *can* or *have to*.**

1 .... I go to Tom's house?

No, ... do your homework.

2 .... you come to the park?

No, ... clean my room.

Reading Record

Book 1
Toy Story 2

This book: ☆ ☆ ☆ ☆ ☆

My favorite part:

I like ...

My new words:

STAMP

Book 2
101 Dalmatians

This book: ☆ ☆ ☆ ☆ ☆

My favorite part:

I like ...

My new words:

STAMP

Book 3
Tangled

This book: ☆ ☆ ☆ ☆ ☆

My favorite part:

I like ...

My new words:

STAMP

Book 4
A Bug's Life

This book: ☆☆☆☆☆

My favorite part:

I like ....
....
....
....

My new words:

....
....
....
....

STAMP

Book 5
Coco

This book: ☆☆☆☆☆

My favorite part:

I like ....
....
....
....

My new words:

....
....
....
....

STAMP

Book 6
Frozen 2

This book: ☆☆☆☆☆

My favorite part:

I like ....
....
....
....

My new words:

....
....
....
....

STAMP

Spelling Practice

Common words	Look and write.	Cover and write.	✔
wasn't			
weren't			
How			
often			
always			
never			
Why			
because			
January			
February			
March			
April			
May			
June			
July			
August			
September			
October			
November			
December			

Comparative adjectives	Look. Write the second word.	Cover and write.	✔
long → long**er**			
tall → tall**er**			
big → big**ger**			
hot → hot**ter**			
funny → funn**ier**			
dirty → dirt**ier**			

Plural nouns	Look. Write the second word.	Cover and write.	✔
star → stars			
eye → eyes			
horse → horses			
glass → glasses			
box → boxes			
puppy → puppies			
leaf → leaves			
Past tense verbs			
like → liked			
watch → watched			
open → opened			
start → started			
stop → stopped			
plan → planned			
try → tried			
carry → carried			
play → played			
enjoy → enjoyed			
***-ing* forms**			
do → doing			
go → going			
help → helping			
wear → wearing			
write → writing			
ride → riding			
sit → sitting			
swim → swimming			

Word List

a

a little
a lot
across
address
afraid
air vent
also
always
ant
apartment
appear
asleep

b

bang
bank
bark
basket
beautiful
because
better
bird
body
bored
born
box
brave
bread
bridge
brush

bug
busy
butterfly
by

c

call
called
camp
candy
car
case
caterpillar
celebrate
centimeter
chair
change
child
circus
city
classmate
climb
colorful
competition
conveyor belt
cool
cookie
costume
count
cowboy
cowgirl

crash
crown
cry
cut

d

dam
dangerous
dead
die
different
difficult
dirt
dirty
disappear
dream
dress
drink

e

earth
electricity
email
escape

f

face paint
fall
fall in love
famous
far

feel
festival
fight
fire
first
floor
flower
fool
forest
forget
frog
fun
fur

g

gang
glacier
glass
gold
golden
grandson
grasshopper
ground
guard
guitar

h

hate
have to
heal
hide

his
hit
hobby
horse
hurt

i

ice
iceberg
inside
into
invite
island

k

kick
kilometer
kindly
king

l

lantern
last
later
leaf
leaves
let's
life
light
long
look for

m

made
magic
many
map
mean
meter
mine
mist
mistake
more
morning
movie
museum
musician

n

nature
need
never
news
next
noisy
north

o

only
out
outside

p

paint
paper
parade
park
party
past
pattern
percent
perform
perhaps
ping
pink
photo
photograph
plan
plane
plant
play
please
poison
poster
pretty
princess
promise
puppy
purple
put

q

queen
question
quick
quickly
quiz

r

ran
ranch
real
rip
river
rub

s

said
same
sand
sandwich
save
scare
scarf
sell
shape
shirt
shoe
shop
short
shout
shrine

sick
singer
sink
size
skate
skeleton
skirt
skull
sky
smash
smart
smell
smile
snow
soccer
sometimes
song
space ranger
spirit
sport
spot
stage
star
stay
stick
store
straight
street
summer
surprised

 t

tear
terrible
than
thief
thieves
think
thought
thousand
through
ticket
tie
tied up
today
together
tomb
tomorrow
tonight
too
top
touch
tower
TV commercial
TV show

 u

use
usually

 v

village
voice

 w

wagon
wake up
wall
wash
weak
week
weight
welcome
west
wet
which
why
wings
without
world
would like

 y

yard
yard sale
year
yes
young
your